CW00727439

Available in Piccolo Books

Kids' London
Kids' Britain
The Piccolo Book of Travelling Games

The Traveller's Quiz Book

●

Deborah Manley

Illustrations by Matthew Doyle

A Piccolo Original
Piccolo Books

First published 1987 by Pan Books Ltd,
Cavaye Place, London SW10 9PG

9 8 7 6 5 4 3 2

© Deborah Manley 1987

Illustrations © Matthew Doyle 1987

ISBN 0 330 29774 0

Photoset by Rowland Phototypesetting Ltd,
Bury St Edmunds, Suffolk
Printed and bound in Great Britain by
Cox & Wyman Ltd, Reading

Whilst the advice and information in this book are believed to
be true and accurate at the time of going to press, neither the author
nor the publisher can accept any legal responsibility or liability
for any errors or omissions that may be made.

CONTENTS

Introduction 7

**Part one:
Out and about**

On the coast 10
On the water 13
On the road 17
On the rails 22
What am I wearing? 24
Animals 25
Colourways 28
Towns, cities, villages 29
Names 33
Questions of sport 37
Who lived where? 38
What's that building? 39
Castles 42
Farming 44
Stories and rhymes 47
Royal Britain 48

**Part two:
Round the regions**

London 52
West Country 61
South of England 65
South East England 67
Thames and Chilterns 70
East Anglia 73
Heart of England 76
East Midlands 80
North West 83
Cumbria 86
North East 89
Northumbria 93
Wales 96
Northern Ireland 100
Off the shores of Scotland 103
Scotland 105
Answers 111

INTRODUCTION

When you are travelling around the country do you like to ask (and find out) where you are, what there is to see there, what happens there, what happened there in the past . . . and many other questions? Or, when you are at home, do you like to ask questions and get the answers? If so, here is the book for you.

If you discover something interesting in this book and want to know more about it, have a look at *Kids' Britain* by Betty Jerman and *Kids' London* by Elizabeth Holt and Molly Perham.

This book is divided into two parts. Part one has general questions on everything from road to rail, from food to sport, and from famous people to famous places. Part two has questions about the various regions of the UK. This section is divided up according to the areas covered by each of the regional tourist boards and there is a map of each area.

One last thing before you set off on your journey. When you are travelling around and learn that Richard III grew up here or George III built this or Queen Elizabeth slept here, do you know exactly when that would have been? Probably not! So on pages 48–9 there are two lists to help you. The first is a quick memory aid to the order of monarchs; the second is a list of the dates of each reign.

● ● ●

Part one:
Out and about

ON THE COAST

· THE SEAS AROUND US ·

1 On this map can you label the seas around the United Kingdom's shores and the names of the ports marked?

English Channel
Irish Sea
Atlantic Ocean
North Sea
Dover
Liverpool
Bristol
Felixstowe
Hull
Southampton

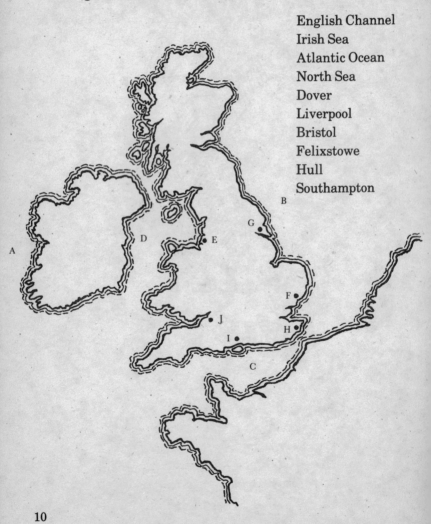

LOOKING OUT
FROM THE COAST

Use the map opposite to answer these questions.

1 Which sea would you be looking at if you were standing on the coast of Suffolk?

2 And if you were standing on the coast of Wales?

3 Which stretch of water runs along the southern coast of Britain?

4 What is it called at its narrowest part?

5 What is the shortest distance from France to England?

6 What expanse of water would you be looking at if you looked west from Land's End?

7 Which country is due east of Great Yarmouth?

8 Which country is due west of Land's End?

· ALONG THE COAST ·

Can you match these coastal features to their definitions?

A	estuary	E	island
B	headland	F	sea loch
C	dunes	G	bay
D	peninsula	H	strait

1 *land surrounded by water*
2 *deep inlets from the sea*
3 *land surrounded by water on three sides*
4 *the wide mouth of a river*
5 *a narrow stretch of water between land*
6 *stretches of sand formed by the wind*
7 *high point of land going out to sea*
8 *part of sea enclosed by wide curve of shore*

· WHAT'S IN THE WASH? ·

Where and what are the following? Match the places to the descriptions.

A The Lizard   **F** The Wash
B The Solway Firth   **G** The Needles
C The Mull of Kintyre   **H** The Solent
D The Butt of Lewis   **I** The Gower Peninsula
E The Minches   **J** The Menai Strait

1 *A peninsula in west Wales*
2 *The bay by Norfolk and Lincolnshire*
3 *The inlet between Cumbria and Scotland*
4 *The channel between the Isle of Wight and the mainland*
5 *The channel between North Wales and Anglesey*
6 *The most southerly headland in Cornwall*
7 *The promontory on a Scottish peninsula*
8 *The channel between mainland Scotland and the Hebrides*
9 *A headland on the Isle of Wight*
10 *The northernmost point of the Hebrides*

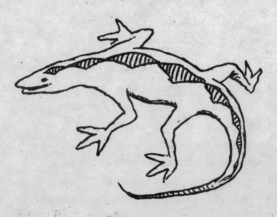

ON THE WATER

· SHIPS AND BOATS ·

1 Which ship sank off Portsmouth in 1545, was raised from the sea in 1982, and is now on show in Portsmouth?

2 What did Sir Francis Drake do in the *Golden Hind* and where can you see a replica of her today?

3 What famous message did Admiral Lord Nelson send to the fleet before the Battle of Trafalgar?

4 She was built by Isambard Kingdom Brunel in Bristol in 1843. She was driven ashore in the Falklands in 1866. She returned to Bristol in 1970 and is now on public display. What is she?

5 Which famous ship was built in Belfast and sank in the Atlantic in 1912?

6 Where in Exeter can you see a steam dredger, rowing boats that have crossed the Atlantic, an Arab dhow and a Hong Kong junk?

7 The television programme *Blue Peter* raised money for an air–sea rescue craft and a lifeboat. Where can you see them?

8 Here is the Blue Peter. What is it?

9 What is a ship's chandler?

10 Which Cornish town is associated with pirates in a musical way?

· CANALS ·

1 What is a lock; a flight of locks; a lock keeper?

2 What is a towpath?

3 Who ran away on a canal tow horse in a famous children's book?

4 What is a barge; a narrow boat; a butty?

5 This is a lift bridge. What does it do?

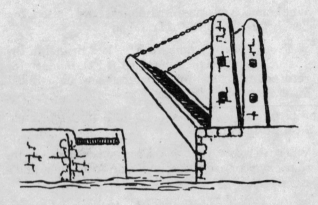

6 What would carry you high up in the air across the River Dee?

7 What canal goes from Manchester to the Mersey?

8 Where is the National Waterways Museum?

9 Which canal links London to Birmingham and Birmingham to Liverpool?

10 Which canal makes it possible to go by water right across Scotland?

· BRIDGES AND CROSSINGS ·

1 What are these?

2 What is this?

3 A packhorse bridge is narrow and quite steep. What was a packhorse?

4 What is a toll bridge?

5 What is a bridge, with high towers from which cables carry the roadway, called?

6 What is a ford; a watersplash?

7 What is the longest road bridge in Britain?

8 What is this bridge across the Thames in London called?

● ● ●

· ALONG THE ROAD ·

1 What are these? Match them to their definitions.

- **A** a penny farthing
- **B** a juggernaut
- **C** a tram
- **D** a jalopy
- **E** a 'Roller'
- **F** a Mini
- **G** a Gentleman of the Road
- **H** a road hog

1 *a highwayman*
2 *a bicycle with one very large wheel and one small one*
3 *a slang word for a Rolls Royce*
4 *a huge lorry*
5 *a sort of bus that goes on tracks and takes its power from an overhead cable. Once very common in most towns.*
6 *an old, rickety car*
7 *a small Rover Group car*
8 *a selfish driver*

2 What is an A road?

3 What is an L-driver?

4 What is an S-bend?

5 What is a Y-junction?

6 Can you match these different roads with their descriptions?

A	a cart track	**D**	a causeway
B	a drove road	**E**	a packhorse route
C	a green lane	**F**	a turnpike road

1 *an unpaved country road*
2 *a road built by a private company who were allowed to charge a fee or toll for its use to get back their investment*
3 *a raised road often across wet or marshy land*
4 *a track made by animals being driven along it*
5 *a road made by the wheels of vehicles*
6 *a road or track made by horses carrying goods in the olden days*

Road Safety

1 What is the order of the change of traffic lights from red to green and back again?

2 What does the amber light mean?

· SIGNS ALONG THE ROAD ·

1 Signs with red circles usually tell you something that you may not do. What do signs in blue circles usually tell you?

2 What do signs in red triangles usually do?

3 What do these road signs say?

A B C

D E

4 What do these ones tell you?

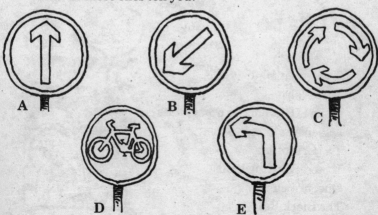

A B C

D E

5 What do these signs warn you of?

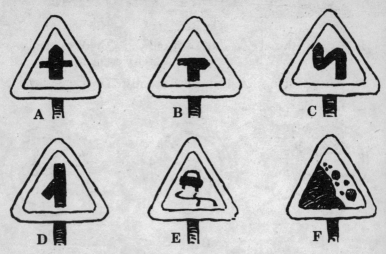

· INNS AND INN SIGNS ·

See how many of these signs you can check off on your travels. Some will be easy to find, others more difficult. Make a note of any unusual ones you see.

The Green Man
Lord Nelson
Duke of Clarence or other Duke
Queen's or King's Arms
The Cricketers
Queen's or King's Head
Queen Victoria
The Black Bull

The Red Lion   The Red Rose
The Lamb   The Woolpack
The Swan   The Bell
The Plough   The Horseshoes

A game to play when you are looking out for inn signs

Form two teams, one for each side of the road. You score for the number of 'legs' on the inn signs on your side of the road. For example, if a pub with the sign 'The Volunteer' is on your side, you score 2 because he has 2 legs, and for the 'Coach and Horses' you score 8 for the legs of both horses. If there are no legs on the sign, as with the 'King's Arms', you take off a point.

● ● ●

ON THE RAILS

· RAILWAYS ·

1 Locomotion 1 was George Stephenson's steam engine. It is on show in Darlington. Where?

2 Where was the first passenger railway line which you can still travel on today?

3 Which bridge in Scotland has 518-metre (1,700 foot)-long main spans and is 110 metres (360 feet) above the Forth? It is said that as soon as they finish painting one end it is time to start at the other again.

4 You'll see these beside a railway line. They are called distance posts. What do they tell you?

5 This is a gradient post. What does it tell the engine driver?

6 What are these? Match them to their definitions.

A	a cutting	D	an embankment
B	a tunnel	E	a viaduct
C	a signal box	F	a goods yard

1 *a place where freight trains are collected and loaded*

2 *a way cut under the ground for a track*

3 *a bridge carrying a road or railway track*

4 *the building by the railway line from which movements of trains are controlled. (This work is increasingly done from central signalling points.)*

5 *a way cut through the ground for the track*

6 *raised ground supporting the track*

· *STATIONS* ·

Can you match the cities with their stations?

1	Liverpool	A	*Temple Meads*
2	London	B	*Piccadilly*
3	Birmingham	C	*Waverley*
4	Bath	D	*Lime Street*
5	Edinburgh	E	*Spa*
6	Bristol	F	*St Pancras*
7	Manchester	G	*New Street*
8	Glasgow	H	*Broadmead*

A game to play

As you leave each station, guess how far it is to the next one and check your guesses against the distance posts.

WHAT AM I WEARING?

Many areas and towns have given their names to articles of clothing and materials. Can you match the place to the article?

1	Glengarry	A	cape
2	Harris	B	type of knitting
3	Inverness	C	cord (or corduroy)
4	Norfolk	D	'bonnet'
5	Guernsey	E	type of shoe
6	Oxford	F	jacket
7	Bedford	G	sweater
8	Ulster	H	tweed
9	Fair Isle	I	coat
10	Cardigan	J	knitted jacket

· DOG-WATCH ·

Can you name these dogs?

· ANIMAL LAND ·

1. What are Friesians, Ayrshires and Guernseys?

2. What are Herefords, Galloways and Lincoln Reds?

3. What are Percherons, Clydesdales and Suffolk Punches?

4. What are Cheviots, Border Leicesters, Cluns, Swaledales and Southdowns?

5. What are Rhode Island Reds, Buff Orpingtons and Leghorns?

6. What are Large Whites, Landraces and Large Blacks?

7. What is a belted cow?

8. There are nine breeds of pony native to the British Isles. How many can you name?

9. Can you name these birds?

E

F

10 A horsefly is a big fly that worries horses. What are these?

    A a horse block

    B a horse radish

    C a horse chestnut

    D a horsetail

● ● ●

COLOURWAYS

1   What is a village green?

2   Where is Greenwich?

3   Who wore the Lincoln Green?

4   Where are the famous white cliffs? Why are they white?

5   Where are Whitechapel and Whitehall?

6   Who might wear Black Watch?

7   What does a blacksmith do?

8   What river does Blackfriars Bridge cross?

9   Where is the Black Country and why is it so named?

10 Where might you find blue john and what is it?

11 What is Wedgwood blue?

12 What is a bluebell?

13 What is an orangery?

14 If you were given a Blenheim Orange, what would you do with it and why?

15 What is a yellowhammer?

16 Who or what was Capability Brown?

17 What are the Red Arrows?

18 Does a Red Admiral have anything to do with the Navy?

19 What city is famed for its red buses?

20 Where might you find a sea pink and why?

● ● ●

TOWNS, CITIES, VILLAGES

· TOWNS AND CITIES ·

1   Which two cities are jointly known as Oxbridge and why?

2   Of which city is it said, 'A church for every week of the year and a pub for every day'?

3   In which city was Peeping Tom struck blind and why?

4   What happens when you are 'sent to Coventry'?

5   In which Buckinghamshire town has a pancake race been held on Shrove Tuesday each year since 1445?

6   Which town is famous for its 158-metre (518-foot)-tall tower, which houses a permanent circus?

7   Which Midlands city has more canals than Venice?

8   What is a Spa Town? Can you name three?

9   What do Lowestoft, Derby, Swansea, Worcester and Bristol have in common?

10 Which is Britain's second city?

11 What Five Towns form the Potteries and Stoke-on-Trent?

12 Why are they so called?

13 Which city is the 'Athens of the North'?

14 Which is the 'Granite City'?

15 Which city is famed for 'jute, jam and journalism'?

16 Can you match the cities in the first row with their famous streets in the second row?

1	London	A	*Princes Street*
2	Edinburgh	B	*The Lanes*
3	Glasgow	C	*The Bull Ring*
4	Brighton	D	*Oxford Street*
5	Oxford	E	*Sauciehall Street*
6	Birmingham	F	*The High*

17 What statue do you expect to
see in Piccadilly Circus?

18 Can you match these items of 'street furniture' to their
descriptions?

A	a spur stone	**F**	cobblestones
B	a bollard	**G**	a manhole
C	a drinking trough	**H**	a gutter
D	a hydrant	**I**	a market cross
E	a pillar box	**J**	a lych gate

1 *a free-standing box for posting letters*
2 *the drain along the edge of a road*
3 *a covered gateway to a churchyard*
4 *a stone protecting the corner of a building from traffic*
5 *a place where horses can drink*
6 *a building marking the place where a market is held*
7 *a hole in the pavement through which workmen reach the
sewers*
8 *an outlet for water used by firemen*
9 *rounded stones used for paving a street*
10 *a stone which stops traffic from passing through an
opening*

· DRAWING PLACES ·

*Here are four towns written in a picture code.
Can you decipher them?*

A

B

C

D

*Now take turns to draw place names and guess
what each other's drawings represent.*

· HOW DO YOU SAY . . . ? ·

*The names of many towns and villages are spelt
one way and pronounced in another, unexpected way.
Here are a few of them. How are they pronounced?*

1 Leominster, Herefordshire
  A Lemster B Lee-min-ster C Le-o-min-ster
  D Le-om-inster

2 Leicester, Leicestershire
  A Leaster B Lester C Lister D Letchester

3 Aldeburgh, Suffolk
  A Orld-brer B Al-de-burg C Ald-bor-o
  D Old-de-burra

4 Yeovil, Somerset
  A Yo-vil B Yee-o-vil C Ye-vil D Yur-vil

5 Norwich, Norfolk
  A Northwich B Nor-wick C Nor-wich
  D Nor-rich

6 Harwich, Essex
  A Ha-rich B Har-wich C Harch D Har-wick

7 Salisbury, Wiltshire
  A Sall-is-bury B Sawls-bury C Sawl-is-bury
  D Sales-bury

8 Taunton, Somerset
  A Torn-ton B Townton C Tarn-ton D Tone-ton

9 Worcester, Worcestershire
  A Wor-chester B Work-ester C Wor-chester
  D Woos-ter

10 Dolgellau, Gwynned
  A Dol-gell-o B Dol-ge-lo C Do-gell-oo
  D Dol-geth-lao

· NAMES AND NICKNAMES ·

1 Where is the Emerald Isle?

2 Where is 'the garden of England'?

3 Where are the Eleanor Crosses? Where is the last such cross?

4 Many surnames come from the occupations or home area of your distant forebears. Some of them, like Smith, Weaver or Thatcher, are easily connected with a trade. Others, like Bedford, Oxford and Kent, are easily connected to a place. Many are more obscure. Can you match these surnames with an occupation?

A	Cooper	**F**	Steward
B	Wright	**G**	Cartwright
C	Mason	**H**	Merchant
D	Baker	**I**	Pedlar
E	Butcher	**J**	Clark

1 *a seller of meat*
2 *a maker of carts and wagons*
3 *a maker of bread*
4 *a travelling salesman*
5 *a maker of wheels, carts or ships, etc.*
6 *a maker of barrels*
7 *a seller of goods*
8 *a writer or clerk*
9 *a stone worker*
10 *someone who looks after another's estate*

5 What does **o'** in Irish names and **ap** in Welsh names mean?

· PLACE NAMES ·

*Many places take their names from their
original site. Some of these names were Old
English, Saxon, Roman, French, Welsh or
Gaelic. If we know a few words in these
languages we can guess something about place
names. But a note of warning: you can't be sure
without checking back into history. Words
change with the centuries and may no longer
mean what they appear to mean!*

1 Before we start looking at place names, do you know what a
prefix is and what a suffix is? If you don't, look at the
answers on pages 115-16.

2 The word BOROUGH or BURY indicated a defended place. Can
you think of three places with these as a prefix or suffix?
Examples: Boroughbridge, Banbury.

3 The word CASTER or CHESTER indicates that a walled Roman
town once stood there. Can you think of three places with
such names? Caister-on-Sea is one.

4 Anglo-Saxon villages have names ending in -ING. Can you
think of three towns or villages in southern England with
this ending?

5 Can you think of three towns or villages with names that
tell you they were built at a ford (a shallow crossing place in
a river)?

6 When places are at the mouth of a river (where it flows into
the sea), they often have the suffix -MOUTH. Can you think
of three such places?

7 The Norse suffix -BY meant village. Can you name three
places with this suffix? Many of them are in Northern
England.

8 The Norse for church was KIRK. What might Kirkby Moor-
side mean?

9 Some county names have curious abbreviations. What are these in full?

A Oxon **B** Salop **C** Glos **D** Northants

10 What is the original meaning of Thames, Avon, Severn and Ouse?

· A MENU OF PLACE NAMES ·

Where can you eat a hotpot?
Can you match these places with the food – or
foods – to which they have given their name?

1	Kendal	**A**	*ham*	**H** *pork pie*
2	Melton Mowbray	**B**	*cheese*	**I** *clotted cream*
3	York	**C**	*sauce*	**J** *rock*
4	Stilton	**D**	*smokies*	**K** *cake*
5	Yorkshire	**E**	*mint cake*	**L** *hotpot*
6	Worcester	**F**	*rum butter*	**M** *tart*
7	Cumberland	**G**	*pudding*	**N** *bloater*
8	Arbroath			
9	Bakewell			
10	Devonshire			
11	Lancashire			
12	Yarmouth			
13	Banbury			
14	Edinburgh			
15	Eccles			

· AN ABC OF PLACE NAMES ·

*Here are 25 clues, each of which will give you –
when you solve it – the name of a place
beginning with the letter of the clue.
Just to set you off, the first answer is given
to you.*

A Sounds like entrance for fruit.   *Appledore*

B Ringer and swift.

C Sounds as if it's arrived and joined a river crosser.

D Do soles come from here?

E Sweet rock does come from here.

F Caretaker for aquatic creatures?

G Top part of garden entrance?

H Famous for the battle of 1066.

I Source of capes?

J Rhymes with a large green vegetable.

K On-Thames or in Jamaica?

L The longest town of all?

M Male castle?

N Not a wizard either . . .

O Exclamation and exclude!

P Town for singing pirates?

Q Female sovereign's river crossing?

R Crimson girl's home?

S Home of Welsh patron saint?

T About 2,000 pounds over the water?

U Take G off seabird and lead it to water.

V An opening neither?

W A city in London.

Y Yeoman's town?

Z Village not far from Land's End as well as alphabet's end.

QUESTIONS OF SPORT

1   Can you match these places to the sport which makes them famous?

    1   Badminton   **A**   *football*
    2   Isle of Man   **B**   *cricket*
    3   Cowes   **C**   *rugby*
    4   Henley   **D**   *horse racing*
    5   Newbury   **E**   *horse trials*
    6   Cardiff Arms Park **F**   *motorbike racing*
    7   Trent Bridge   **G**   *sailing*
    8   Brand's Hatch   **H**   *rowing*
    9   Wimbledon   **I**   *car racing*
   10   Anfield   **J**   *tennis*

2   What have these places in common?
   Newmarket;   Thirsk;   Newton Abbot

3   To which city does each of these football teams belong?

    A   Albion   **E**   North End
    B   Wednesday   **F**   Athletic
    C   Rovers   **G**   Wanderers
    D   Forest   **H**   Thistle

4   What happens at Henley-on-Thames in June?

5   What takes place between Putney and Mortlake?

6   Why is Hambledon, near Portsmouth, known as 'the cradle of cricket'?

7   What is the Grand National and where does it happen?

8   What is the origin of steeplechasing?

9   What links Trent Bridge, Lord's and The Oval?

10   Who are the following?:

    A   the Canaries   **D**   the Saints
    B   the Hammers   **E**   the Gunners
    C   the Toffees   **F**   Hibs

WHO LIVED WHERE?

*Many of the houses where great and famous
people lived are now open to the public.
Do you know who lived in which place?*

1   Benjamin Disraeli, Prime Minister and novelist
2   Jane Austen, novelist
3   George Bernard Shaw, playwright
4   William Wordsworth, poet
5   The Brontë sisters, novelists
6   Beatrix Potter, author
7   James Barrie, playwright and author
8   Robert Burns, poet
9   Rudyard Kipling, author
10 Anna Sewell, author of Black Beauty

A   *Dove Cottage, Grasmere*
B   *Kirriemuir, Angus,
     Tayside*
C   *Hughenden Manor, Bucks*
D   *Haworth Parsonage, West
     Yorks*
E   *Batemans, West Sussex*
F   *Chawton, Hants*
G   *Church Plain, Great
     Yarmouth*
H   *Ayot St Lawrence, Herts*
I   *Alloway, Strathclyde*
J   *Hilltop, Sawrey, Cumbria*

WHAT'S THAT BUILDING?

1 This is a toll house. What is it used for?

2 This is an oast house. What is it and where would you be most likely to see it?

3 The keep is a part of what sort of building?

4 What is a folly when it is a building?

5 What is this building in Stoke-on-Trent? Once there were many of them all over the town, but now only a few remain.

6 What are these and on what site would you see them?

7 Where might winding gear like this be seen?

8 Where might you see a skyline like this?

9 Which of these is a tower mill and which is a post mill?

A

B

10 What does this building do?

CASTLES

1 Can you match the terms for various parts of a castle to their definitions?

A	moat	**F**	curtain wall
B	keep	**G**	turret
C	drawbridge	**H**	portcullis
D	dungeon	**I**	garderobes
E	bailey	**J**	barbican

1 *a small tower*
2 *door which slid down in grooves*
3 *toilets set into the wall*
4 *outer defence to defend gatehouse*
5 *main tower of a castle*
6 *bridge which could be raised or lowered across a moat*
7 *outer wall around a castle*
8 *area within the castle wall*
9 *prison underground*
10 *water filled ditch around a castle*

2 How many medieval stone castles are there in England and Wales?

 A 100–200 **B** 300–400 **C** 400–600
 D nearly 1,000

3 In which castle is there the keep known as the White Tower?

4 Which castle is known as 'the Key of England'?

5 Which castle is now occupied by the offices of the Royal Observatory?

6 Which Cornish castle is linked with the legend of King Arthur?

7 Which is the oldest inhabited castle in Britain?

8 Which castle is owned by Madame Tussaud's?

9 What is the link between Prince Charles and Caernarfon Castle?

10 This Welsh castle had one tower blasted in the 1600s and has been leaning over since. What is it called?

• • •

1 Can you identify these farm machines and equipment?

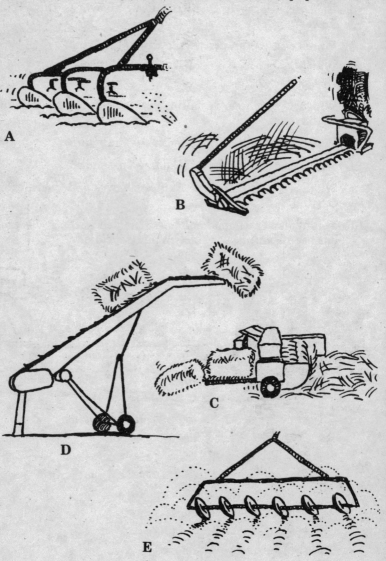

A

B

C

D

E

2 Can you match up some of the machines with the following definitions?

1 *breaks up clods of earth*
2 *cuts grass for hay*
3 *breaks up earth to prepare land for sowing*
4 *lifts bales to top of haystack*
5 *sprays crops to kill insects, etc.*
6 *makes hay into bales and ties them with string*
7 *breaks up and turns over earth*
8 *pulls the other farm equipment*
9 *reaps and threshes the grain*
10 *turns the hay to dry it out*

3 What is this sort of barn called?

4 What are fertilizers?

5 What is a byre?

6 What is irrigation?

7 What happens in a dairy parlour?

8 What is a dry-stone wall?

9 What is this and what is it used for on a farm?

10 What is a silo?

A game to play

Score a point for each item of farm machinery you identify on your journey.

STORIES AND RHYMES

1   Can you match the book and the area or place with which it is associated?

A	Northanger Abbey	F	Lorna Doone
B	Cranford	G	Kidnapped
C	Peter Pan	H	The Mayor of Casterbridge
D	Pigeon Post	I	Sherlock Holmes
E	Wuthering heights	J	Swallows and Amazons

1	*The Broads*	6	*Glencoe, Scotland*
2	*Bath*	7	*Knutsford, Cheshire*
3	*The Lake District*	8	*Dorchester*
4	*Baker Street, London*	9	*West Riding moors*
5	*North Devon*	10	*Kensington Gardens, London*

2   In which Yorkshire village is Dickens' model for Dotheboys Hall in *Nicholas Nickleby*?

3   Where was a tailor helped by mice?

4   Where did Robin Hood and his Merry Men live? Their enemy was the Sheriff of which city?

5   In which West Country village, known as the prettiest village in England, was *The Story of Dr Doolittle* filmed?

6   Who lived in Batemans in Sussex and set his/her book *Puck of Pook's Hill* in the surrounding country?

7   Where is the original of *Bleak House*, where Charles Dickens wrote *David Copperfield*?

8   Samuel Johnson, the great lexicographer, was born in Lichfield in Staffordshire. What is a lexicographer?

9   Which three famous writers, all women, grew up in the parsonage at Haworth?

10 Where did Christopher Robin go with Alice?

ROYAL BRITAIN

*Here is a ridiculous rhyme to help you remember
the kings and queens of Britain from William
the Conqueror to George VI!*

Willie, Willie, Harry, Stee,
Harry, Dick, John, Harry Three,
One, Two, Three Neds, Richard Two,
Harry Four, Five, Six. Then who?
Edward Four, Five, Dick the Bad,
Harrys twain and Nick the Lad,
Mary, Bessie, James the Vain,
Charlie, Charlie, James again,
William and Mary, Anna Gloria,
Four Georges, William, and Victoria.
Edward Seventh next, and then
George the Fifth in 1910.
Edward the Eighth soon abdicated
And so a George was reinstated.

William I (the Conqueror)
1066–87

William II (Rufus)
1087–1100

Henry I 1100–35

Stephen 1135–54 (Civil War
with Empress Mathilda
1139–53)

Henry II 1154–89 (first
Plantaganet)

Richard I (Cœur de Lion)
1189–99

John 1199–1216

Henry III 1216–72

Edward I 1272–1307

Edward II 1307–27

Edward III 1327–77

Richard II 1377–99

Henry IV 1399–1413
(first Lancastrian)

Henry V 1413–22

Henry VI 1422–61

Edward IV 1461–83
(first Yorkist)

Edward V April to June
1483

Richard III 1483–5

Henry VII 1485–1509
(first Tudor)

Henry VIII 1509–47

Edward VI 1547–53

Mary 1553–8

Elizabeth I 1558–1603

James I (James VI of
Scotland, first Stuart)
1603–25

Charles I 1625–49

The Commonwealth and
Protectorate under Oliver
Cromwell 1649–60

Charles II 1660–85

James II 1685–8

William III of Orange and
Mary 1689–1702

Anne 1702–14

George I 1714–27
(first Hanoverian)

George II 1727–60

George III 1760–1820

George IV 1820–30

William IV 1830–7

Victoria 1837–1901

Edward VII 1901–10

George V 1910–36 (first
House of Windsor)

Edward VIII 1936
(abdicated)

George VI 1936–52

Elizabeth II 1952–

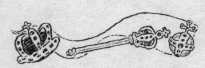

Now answer these questions on Royal Britain.

1   Who is the Duke of Cornwall?

2   There is a hillfort in Somerset which is reputed to be the site of King Arthur's Camelot. Where is it?

3   Where is Arthur, 'The Once and Future King', said to be buried?

4   At which castle in Dorset was the Saxon king Edward murdered in AD 978?

5   Another king met his end here! The Rufus Stone near Culham in the New Forest marks the spot where an English Norman king was killed in 1100. Who was he and how did he die?

6   What school in Berkshire was founded by King Henry IV in 1440 and is still a school today?

7   Who built Windsor Castle and who lives there now?

8   Which Queen has her dolls' house on display at Windsor?

9   Where was Prince Charles invested as Prince of Wales?

10   Where was the first Prince of Wales born and how was he given to the Welsh as their prince?

11   Which English king was born in Monmouth and is commemorated in the town by Agincourt Square?

12   What creature is linked with the Scottish King Robert the Bruce because he learned persistence from it?

13   At which abbey was Robert the Bruce buried?

14   James VI of Scotland built it and it is now the official residence of the monarch in Scotland. What is it?

15   Where was Princess Margaret born?

● ● ●

Part two:
Round the regions

· PLACES ·

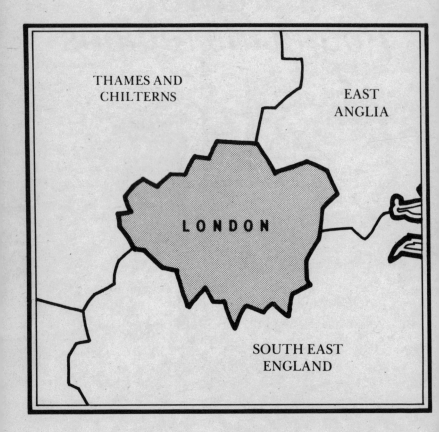

1 From where is it thought that Romans measured distances from London? Where are distances measured from today?

2 What and where is the house known as Number One, London?

3 Where, in Covent Garden, can you see theatrical costumes, sets and memorabilia?

4 Where can you see the sun, moon and stars in the daytime in central London?

5 Why was the Cenotaph in Whitehall built?

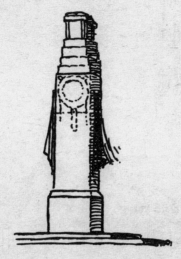

6 What and where is the world's largest toyshop?

7 Where can you see what makes a volcano explode or a mountain range rise up?

8 Where was the first Punch and Judy show?

9 What do you see in the Costume Hall of the Victoria and Albert Museum?

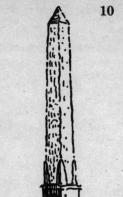

10 Cleopatra's Needle stands on the Embankment. What is it?

11 Where would you go to see a Palm House, and a Chinese Pagoda set in beautiful gardens?

12 What do you need to have heard when you were born to call yourself a real Cockney? What is a Cockney?

● ● ●

· ROYAL LONDON ·

1 It was built by William the Conqueror and has been a royal residence, a prison, a mint and an observatory. What is it?

2 What jewels can be seen there?

3 Which museum stands on the site of the royal palace of Placentia, where Queen Elizabeth I was born?

4 Where is the Coronation Chair?

5 Where does Richard the Lion Heart raise his sword today?

6 Who rides in a chariot with her daughters beside the Thames?

7 Which palace was given to Henry VIII by Cardinal Wolsey?

8 Which king's statue looks down Whitehall to where he died on the scaffold?

9 It houses the Gold State Coach, the Irish State Coach and the Glass Coach. What and where is it? What are the coaches used for?

10 How can you tell that the Sovereign is in residence at Buckingham Palace?

11 Where do Guards troop their 'colour' in front of the Queen on her official birthday? What is the 'colour'?

12 Where can you visit the rooms where Queen Victoria lived when she was a child?

· LONDON'S RIVER ·

1 How many bridges are there across the Thames in Greater London?

   A 3   B 6   C 12   D 25   E 17

2 Can you name two of them?

3 How many tunnels are there under the Thames in the same area?

A 3   **B** 6   **C** 12   **D** 25   **E** 17

4 Can you name two of them?

5 Where can you walk under the Thames?

6 Where is the London Bridge of the nursery rhyme? Has it fallen down?

7 Which bridge can open to allow ships through?

8 Where can you learn about London's bridges?

9 Where and what is the Thames Barrier?

10 Where, near Tower Bridge, can you visit a collection of historic ships?

11 Where do *Jason* and *Jenny Wren* take you?

12 What and where is HMS *Belfast*?

13 What and where are the *Cutty Sark* and *Gypsy Moth II*?

14 What would you go to see at the National Maritime Museum at Greenwich?

15 Which river snakes through Kensington Gardens and Hyde Park?

● ● ●

· LONDON'S TRANSPORT ·

1　Where can you see the history of London's public transport?

2　Where are Puffing Billy, the Rocket and the Caerphilly Castle housed together?

3　What do Victoria, Waterloo and Euston have in common?

4　What is said to be the world's busiest railway junction?

5　Where in London might you see the Fokker E-1, Handley Page 0/400 and a V2, and what are they?

6　What do Hurricanes, Mosquitoes and Spitfires have in common, and where in London can you see them?

7　If you were travelling about London, what form of transport would you be going on if you travelled on a Number 11, Number 15 and Number 8?

8　What is the nickname for the London underground?

A	the metro	**C**	the tube
B	the subway	**D**	the railway

• • •

· LONDON'S PEOPLE ·

1 If you see a blue plaque like this on a building in London, what does it tell you?

2 Who lived in these houses? Can you match the house to the person?

    A 1 Gough Square, off Fleet Street

    B Wentworth House, NW3

    C 47 City Road, EC1

    D 48 Doughty Street, WC1

  1 *Charles Dickens*   3 *Dr Samuel Johnson*

  2 *John Keats*   4 *John Wesley*

3 Where did Dick Whittington turn again and so become Lord Mayor of London?

4 Who lives in the Mansion House?

5   Who is the Old Lady of Threadneedle Street?

6   Who are the ancient giants of London who live in the Guildhall and guard the City?

7   Who guards the Tower of London?

8   Where can you see famous people and replicas of Britain's nastier crimes?

9   What do these people have in common?
Thomas Hardy, Geoffrey Chaucer, William Shakespeare, Charles Dickens

10 Who lived in Kensington Gardens and can still be seen playing his pipes there today?

· LONDON'S ANIMALS ·

1   Where can you see a panda, lions and orang-utans in the middle of London?

2   Which birds live in the Tower of London and are officially fed there?

3   Where can you see soldiers on horseback in Whitehall?

4   Where will you meet dinosaurs, the dodo and a huge whale?

5   Which famous birds live in St James's Park?

6 Where do dinosaurs peer at you from islands in a lake in south London?

7 What is the South Bank Lion?

8 Which creatures lie around the foot of Nelson's Column in Trafalgar Square?

· *LONDON LANDMARKS* ·

1 What marks the spot in Pudding Lane where the Great Fire of London broke out in 1666? How many steps are there in it?

2 Trinidad, Tanzania and Tonga are all on exhibition here. Where is it?

3 What and where is the Greenwich Meridian?

4 What is Sadler's Wells?

5 Which museum has a superb collection of dolls, dolls' houses, rocking-horses and toy soldiers?

6 Where can you meet teddy bears and go on a miniature train ride in London?

7 Which Corporation links Portland Place and White City?

8 What area does the City of London cover?

9 What is Fleet Street famous for and what is it named after?

10 Which market once sold flowers, fruit and vegetables but is now a general shopping area?

11 What great event for gardeners is held each year in the grounds of the Royal Hospital?

12 What is Petticoat Lane?

13 What links White Hart Lane and Stamford Bridge?

14 Who gives London the Christmas tree which stands each year in Trafalgar Square? Why?

WEST COUNTRY

In this section there are questions about Cornwall, Devon, Somerset, Wiltshire and Avon.

1 Which waters surround Cornwall?

2 How far is it from Land's End to John o' Groats?
  A 500 miles
  B 900 miles
  C 1,000 miles
  D 1,200 miles

3 In which county is tin mined?

4 What do Polperro, Looe and Mevagissey have in common?

5 How do you spell the name of the Cornish village pronounced Mouzel?

6 What is a Piskey?

7 Where is an annual floral dance held?

8 Where can you see Buckingham Palace, the White House, the Leaning Tower of Pisa and Stonehenge all at once?

9 Where is the only butterfly museum in Britain?

10 What happened at Helston in Cornwall in 1901 which linked Britain, American and Italy?

11 This is a Stargazy pie. What is it made of?

12 Where were Bill Brewer, Jan Stewer, Peter Gurney, Peter Davey, Dan'l Whiddon and others going?

13 What does the Mayflower Stone in Plymouth commemorate, and who were the Pilgrim Fathers?

14 What would you travel on and where would you go if you bought a ticket on the Dart Valley Railway?

15 Where is a cliff railway hauled up the cliff by water tanks?

16 Which castle is known as King Arthur's castle?
   A St Michael's Mount
   B Windsor
   C Tintagel

17 In which county is the birthplace of Axminster carpets?

18 Which Devon town is famed for its lace?
   A Exeter
   B Tiverton
   C Bude
   D Honiton

19 What is Dunkery Beacon on Exmoor?
   A a hotel
   B a high point
   C a fire station
   D a village

20 What career would you have chosen if you were studying at Dartmouth? Why?

21 For what drink is Somerset renowned?

22 Wookey Hole is famed for its caves with stalactites and stalagmites. Which go up and which go down?

23 Where can you climb Jacob's Ladder in Somerset and what will you see when you reach the top?

24 Where are 200 famous heads stored and why?

25 What gives Bath its name?

26 Where near Bath can you see American patchwork quilts, Indian tepees and eat brownies?

27 Which suspension bridge built by Isambard Kingdom Brunel, the great Victorian engineer, spans the Avon Gorge?

28 Poulteney Bridge in Bath has three arches and shops along the bridge. Which river does it span?

29 What is the town of Wilton famous for, giving its name to?
    A   cheese
    B   carpets
    C   leatherwork
    D   marmalade

30 Where can you see Concorde 002 and other historic aircraft?

• • •

SOUTH OF ENGLAND

In this section there are questions about Dorset, Hampshire and the Isle of Wight.

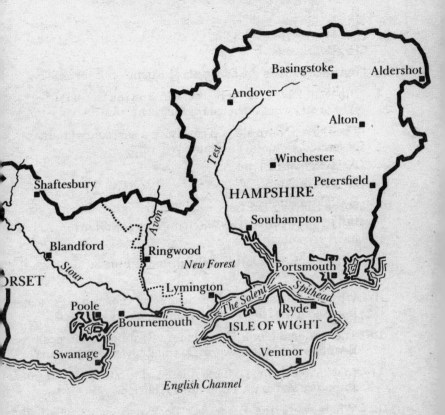

1 Badbury Rings are near Wimborne in Dorset. What are they?

2 Over 100 tanks but no war. Where might you be?

3 Near which town did Mary Annan find fossils and where may you still find fossils in the cliffs today?
   A Dorchester
   B Swanage
   C Lyme Regis
   D Bournemouth

4 In which town is the Dinosaur Museum?

5 Dinosaur footprints were discovered on the Isle of Purbeck. Where and what is the Isle of Purbeck?

6 The Dorset Naturalists' Trust have a sanctuary for ducks, geese and swans on an island. Where?
   A Brownsea Island
   B Isle of Wight
   C Isle of Purbeck

7 What do Spettisbury, Witchampton and Newton Abbas have in common?

8 Where did Sir Walter Raleigh build himself a house in 1594?

9 Why will you see horses, ponies, cows and even pigs roaming free in the New Forest? What is the New Forest?

10 The National Motor Museum is at Beaulieu in Hampshire. Beaulieu is a French word. Do you know what it means?

11 In which cathedral is Jane Austen, the author of *Pride and Prejudice* and many other novels, buried?

12 Where were the Domesday Book documents originally stored? What is the Domesday Book?

13 There is only one military camp in Britain which was built since Roman times. Where is it?

14 In which 'army' town can you see the history of the British Army since 1854?

15 Which is the home port of the QE2? What is she?

SOUTH EAST ENGLAND

In this section there are questions on Surrey, West and East Sussex and Kent.

1 What and where are the South Downs? What is named after them?

2 What international airport lies in West Sussex?
   A Heathrow
   B Gatwick
   C Stansted
   D Northolt

3 What is to be built from near Folkestone to France? How will you travel through it?

4 By what forms of transport do people cross the Channel?

5 Which county is known as 'the Garden of England'?

6 This is one of the oldest white horses cut in the chalky hillsides all over England. What is it called?

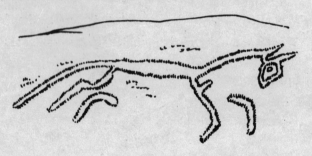

7 What happened at Runnymede in 1215?

8 What did this give the British people?

9 What is the Hog's Back?
   A a ridge in Surrey
   B a down in Sussex
   C a weald in Kent
   D a valley in Surrey

10 Where are the Royal Horticultural Society's gardens? What is horticulture?

11   Where is the Royal Military College, where army officers are trained?

     A   Aldershot

     B   Colchester

     C   Brighton

     D   Sandhurst

12   Which palace in Brighton was built by the Prince Regent in oriental style?

13   Where in Brighton can you see over 100 penny slot machines?

14   William the Conqueror vowed that should the victory be his, he would build an abbey to thank God. Which abbey did he build?

15   What has the Bayeux Tapestry to do with England?

16   What do you see at the Dolphinarium in Brighton?

17   What was fought from Biggin Hill over the skies of Britain?

18   Which castle once guarded a harbour which is now silted up?

     A   Pevensey

     B   Deal

     C   Rye

     D   Herstmonceux

19   Which railway line runs miniature trains across the Romney marshes?

20   What is the Pilgrim's Way?

●   ●   ●

THAMES AND CHILTERNS

The questions in this section cover Berkshire, Buckinghamshire, Hertfordshire and Oxfordshire.

1 What are the Chilterns?

   A a series of lakes

   B a range of hills

   C a breed of local cattle

   D a type of building

2 What is the Ridgeway Path that runs through this area?

3 Where in Reading can you see portraits of livestock and beekeeping equipment among many other exhibits?

4 Who was the Iron Duke who lived at Stratfield Saye, near Reading, and at Number One, London?

5 The Duke of Marlborough's ancestor was given this house by the nation in 1705. Which Prime Minister was born here?

6 Which river did Jerome K. Jerome's three men travel in their boat?

7 Which library in Oxford has over three million volumes, dating from the sixteenth century?

8 What and where in Oxford is Old Tom?

9 One of Oxford's colleges is called Magdalen. How do you pronounce it?

   A Mag-dal-en

   B Maudlin

   C Mag-dal-ane

   D Mayg-dar-len

10 Where would you have gone to see a fine lady upon a white horse?

11 What cakes have been made in the same shop in Banbury since 1608?

12 Which is the oldest museum in England?

13 Which is the oldest model village, dating from 1929?

14 What is the country home of London Zoo?

15 Which animal can you see from miles away before you reach the Zoo?

16 Where do historic aircraft fly on display?

   A the Shuttleworth Collection

   B Heathrow Airport

   C Bedford Museum

   D Stansted Airport

17 Where do buffalo roam in the grounds of a country house?

18 In which great country house in Hertfordshire did Queen Elizabeth I hear that she had become Queen of England?

● ● ●

EAST ANGLIA

The area known as East Anglia includes Essex, Cambridgeshire, Suffolk and Norfolk.

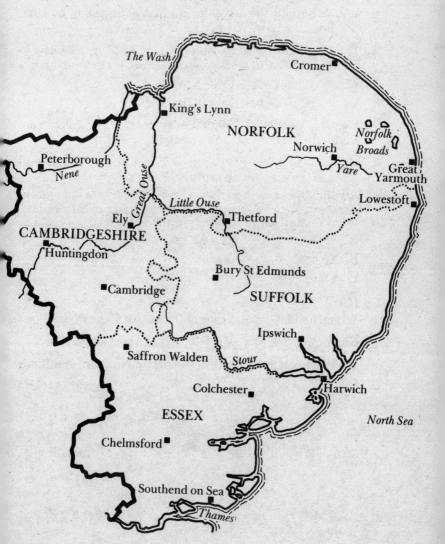

1 Which is the nearest forest to London?

2 It is Britain's oldest recorded town, once called Camulodunum. What is it called today?

3 On the race course of which Suffolk town are the Cambridgeshire and the Caesarewitch run?

4 Which Suffolk town has for its motto 'Shrine of a King, Cradle of the Law'? Why?

5 Thomas Gainsborough was born in 1727 in a house in Sudbury where his work is now on show. What is he famous for?

6 What are the Deben and the Orwell?

7 Why do people who have never been there know East Bergholt, Flatford Mill and Dedham by sight?

8 At Polstead, what happened to Maria Marten in the Red Barn in the nineteenth century?

9 What are the Broads?

10 What roofing material comes from the Broads?
   A tiles
   B thatch
   C slate
   D reeds

11 Which holiday town stands at the mouth of the River Yare?

12 Caister-on-Sea was built long ago as a port – by whom?

13 What connection is there between Church Plain and Black Beauty?

14 Houghton Hall near King's Lynn was built for Sir Robert Walpole. He was a famous 'first'. Why?

15 Which scented flowers are grown commercially in Norfolk?

16 Gonville and Caius is one of the Cambridge colleges. How do you pronounce Caius?

   A Ky-us

   B Keys

   C Cee-us

   D Kay-us

17 Which defensive bank and ditch was built in prehistoric times and runs for seven miles beside the A11 in Cambridgeshire?

18 We have all seen sundials. At which Cambridge college is there a moon dial?

   A Trinity

   B Queen's

   C Downing

   D Gonville and Caius

19 King John was said to have lost his clothes in the Wash when his ship ran aground there. What and where is the Wash?

20 Its nickname is the Fitzbilly. It is in Cambridge. What is it?

● ● ●

HEART OF ENGLAND

The counties which come within the description Heart of England, meaning the central part, are Gloucestershire, Hereford and Worcestershire, Staffordshire, Warwickshire and within this the city of Birmingham.

1 What are the Cotswolds?

2 Which river passes through Shropshire, Hereford and Worcester and Gloucestershire on its way to the sea?

3 What is immediately to the west of the Heart of England?

4 On which river is Shakespeare's birthplace?

5 What and where is the Forest of Dean?

6 What and where is Wenlock Edge?
   A a hill in Worcestershire
   B a valley in Staffordshire
   C an escarpment in Shropshire
   D a ridge in Herefordshire

7 Why do people visit the Vale of Evesham in spring?

8 What is Malvern Water?
   A a lake
   B spring water
   C a river
   D soda water

9 Which canal links Birmingham to the Mersey?

10 Where is the National Exhibition Centre?

11 Which Gloucestershire village was described by the writer and designer William Morris as the most beautiful in England?
   A Bibury
   B Fairford
   C Birdlip
   D Stow-on-the-wold

12 Who lived at College Court, Gloucester with his cat Simpkin?

13 Where is the world's largest collection of wildfowl?

14 A spring flows out into a meadow called Tewkesbury Mead near the village of Coates in Gloucestershire. What does it become?

15 Which Worcestershire village is known as the show village of England?

   A Ombersley

   B Atch Lench

   C Bredon

   D Broadway

16 In which National Trust property can you see a strange collection including old farm implements and Japanese armour?

   A Snowshill

   B Hidcote

   C Charlcote

   D Belvoit

17 Which cathedral has the largest chained library in the world? What is a chained library?

18 Where was the first iron bridge built in 1877–9?

19 Why is Ironbridge called the 'cradle of the Industrial Revolution'?

20 Where does Madame Tussaud exhibit in Warwickshire?

21 Which fortress was described by Sir Walter Scott in his novel of the same name?

22 Whose home town does the Birthplace Trust care for and what is the town?

23 What happens at the Memorial Theatre, Stratford-upon-Avon?

24 Which art gallery houses a magnificent collection of Pre-Raphaelite paintings?

25 Which cathedral is the only one in Britain with three stone spires, known as the Ladies of the Vale?

26 Where do you find a magnificent historic garden combined with fairground rides?

27 Where can you go 213 metres (700 feet) under the ground to see coalmining techniques?

28 In which city are the famous Royal Doulton, Spode and Wedgwood porcelain factories?

29 Which most famous of all anglers lived at Shallowford in Staffordshire?

30 Can you match the first part of these towns with the last part?

A	Kidder	**1**	*ford*
B	Shrews	**2**	*cester*
C	Ciren	**3**	*minster*
D	Staf	**4**	*hampton*
E	Wolver	**5**	*bury*

● ● ●

EAST MIDLANDS

*In this section there are questions about places
in Derbyshire, Leicestershire, Lincolnshire,
Northamptonshire and Nottinghamshire.*

1 What is Europe's largest artificial lake?

2 Which county has been absorbed into Leicestershire?

3 Which county grows more bulbs than the whole of Holland?

4 Where in Derbyshire is the National Tramway Museum?
   A Matlock
   B Crich
   C Derby
   D Ripley

5 How do you reach the Heights of Abraham from Matlock Bath railway station?

6 What do you find when you reach the Heights?

7 Of what mansion was it said, 'all windows, no wall', and why?

8 What have these in common?
   Chee; Dove; Monsal; Water-cum-Jolly

9 What do Bath and Buxton have in common?

10 Who first used water power to drive a cotton mill and used the invention at Comford Old Mill?

11 Which Derbyshire town has a famous crooked spire to its church?

12 What draws speleologists to the Peak District?
    A rocks
    B climbing
    C caves
    D walking

13 Which house near Stamford was built by William Cecil in 1587 and has been lived in by his descendants ever since? Which famous equestrian event takes place there each year?

14 Where is there a spectacular flower parade in the spring?

15 Which flowers is the Spalding area famous for?

16 Which cathedral was shattered by an earthquake and rebuilt in the twelfth and thirteenth centuries?
    A Nottingham
    B Lincoln
    C Derby
    D Birmingham

17 The Boston Stump is a well-known Lincolnshire landmark. What is it?

18 Which law of nature did Isaac Newton discover at Woolathorpe Manor in Lincolnshire?

19 Who was born at 8a Victoria Street, Eastwood and used that area of Derbyshire as the background to his novels?

20 For which material is Nottingham famous?
    A lace
    B leather
    C canvas
    D velvet

NORTH WEST

In this section there are questions about Lancashire and Cheshire and the Isle of Man.

1   What is the Mersey?

2   Which range of hills divides north west England from north east England?
    A   The Grampians
    B   The Quantocks
    C   The Cotswolds
    D   The Pennines

3   How can you cross the Mersey over and under the water?

4   Where is the story of the Beatles told in words and music?

5   Which city has two cathedrals built in this century?

6   Lancashire was the centre of the textile industry in the nineteenth century. Where can you see the history of that industry on display today?

7   What has Port Sunlight to do with soap?

8   Brighton is in Sussex. Where is New Brighton?

9   Sir Alec Rose went round the world in *Lively Lady*. Where can you see her today?

10 What happens at Jodrell Bank?
    A   Money is minted.
    B   There is a famous radio telescope.
    C   It is a centre for motorcycle races.
    D   There is a huge ski slope.

11 Of what place is this the emblem?

12 What is special about a Manx cat?

13 What is the Isle of Man parliament called?
   A House of Commons
   B The Tynwald
   C The Senate
   D The Parlement

14 What is the Lady Isabella on the Isle of Man and what makes it unique?

15 What are Goodison Park and Anfield?

16 The Wars of the Roses were fought long ago. The Rose of Yorkshire was white. What colour was the Rose of Lancashire?

● ● ●

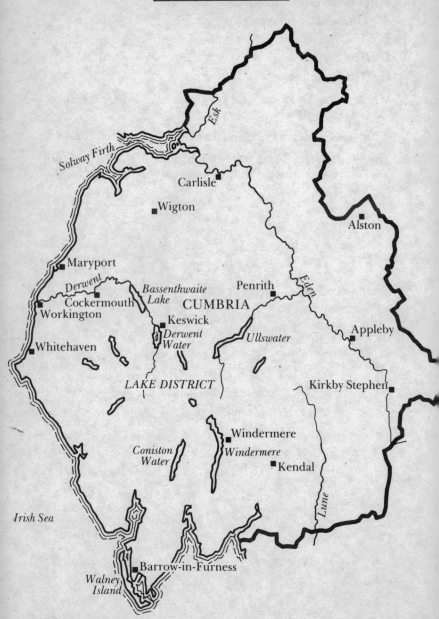

CUMBRIA

Esk

Solway Firth

Carlisle

Wigton

Alston

Maryport

Derwent

Bassenthwaite Lake

Penrith

Eden

Cockermouth

CUMBRIA

Workington

Keswick

Derwent Water

Whitehaven

Ullswater

Appleby

LAKE DISTRICT

Kirkby Stephen

Windermere

Coniston Water

Windermere

Kendal

Irish Sea

Lune

Barrow-in-Furness

Walney Island

1 Which river flows from Derwentwater to the sea?

2 Can you name three lakes in the Lake District?

3 What have Skiddaw, Great Gable, Pillar and Great Dod in common?

4 Which is the biggest lake in England?

5 Which is the deepest lake in England?

6 What is Helvellyn?

7 Who is the Old Man of Coniston?

8 At which castle was Catherine Parr, the last of Henry VIII's wives, born?

9 Where did Tabitha Twitchett go shopping and what is it today?

10 Where can you watch Laurel and Hardy all day long?

11 What was Donald Campbell's boat, in which he gained the water speed record, called?
   A Bluebell
   B Bluebird
   C Blue Arrow
   D Blue Water

12 Who or what were the Swallows and Amazons and what links them to the Lake District?

13 Which Cumbrian city became English in 1092?
   A Carlisle
   B Kendal
   C Barrow in Furness
   D Appleby

14 What are English Gate, Scotch Gate and Irish Gate?

15 What are sold in Kirkby Stephen at the Cowper Day Fair in late September?

A sheep

B ponies

C horses

D cows

16 Where can you see *Dolly*, the oldest mechanically powered boat in the world?

17 How does Sealink cross Windermere?

18 Who are Jeremy Fisher, John Joiner and Benjamin Bunny?

● ● ●

NORTH EAST

In this section there are questions about Humberside and Yorkshire.

1   Which line of hills separates north west and north east England?

2   What is a dale; a fell?

3   In which Humberside city did William Wilberforce, the campaigner against slavery, live?
    A   Hull
    B   Halifax
    C   Grimsby
    D   Beverley

4   Which famous bridge links Humberside with Lincoln?

5   What links a town in Humberside to a town in Nova Scotia, Canada?

6   Can you name three Yorkshire Dales?

7   What is the Pennine Way?

8   What is the highest large freshwater lake in England called?

9   What is Pen-y-Ghent?
    A   a fell
    B   a dale
    C   a village
    D   a church

10 Which three peaks have to be reached in the Three Fells Race?

11 This is the Ribblehead Viaduct. What is it?

12 Why is Tan Hill Inn so famous?

13 Which breed of dog and which breed of sheep take their names from Yorkshire Dales?

14 With which metal is Sheffield especially linked?
    A gold
    B silver
    C iron
    D steel

15 Which castle is renowned for its views along the Swale?
    A Richmond
    B Middleham
    C Barnard
    D Helmsley

16 Which abbey do you approach through the grounds of Studley Royal near Ripon?

17 What have these in common?
Rievaulx; Jervaulx; Easby

18 What have these in common?
Middleham; Pickering; Helmsley; Richmond

19 Who defeated whom at Stamford Bridge in 1066?

20 Which great house has the largest privately owned collection of costume in England?

21 In which house can you see about 10,000 items of miniature furniture in tiny rooms?

22 Where can you be entertained by flamingoes, gnomes and performing parrots?

23 Where can you travel on a railway built by George Stephenson in the 1830s?

24 Which cathedral has the major part of England's stained glass?

  A Durham

  B York

  C Lincoln

  D Canterbury

25 Which famous highwayman is linked to York? Where is the story of York told in the prison where he lay?

• • •

NORTHUMBRIA

The questions in this section cover County Durham and Northumberland.

Berwick-upon-Tweed

Tweed

Holy Island

Alnwick ■

Cheviot Hills

Coquet

North Sea

NORTHUMBERLAND

North Tyne

Morpeth ■

South Tyne

North Shields

Newcastle upon Tyne

South Shields

Hexham ■

Tyne

Gateshead

TYNE AND WEAR ■

Pennines

Sunderland ■

Durham ■

Wear

DURHAM

Hartlepool ■

Bishop Auckland ■

Tees

Stockton-on-Tees ■

Middlesbrough ■

Darlington ■

CLEVELAND

1 What runs from the Solway Firth to Wallsend in southern Northumberland, and what was it built for?

2 What are Housteds and Chesters?

3 Where is there a major new museum devoted to the life of the Roman soldier?

4 Which range of hills forms the 'frontier' with Scotland?

5 Which two rivers join to make up the River Tyne?

6 What is High Force renowned for?

7 What was described as 'half church of God, half castle 'gainst the Scot'?

8 In Durham Cathedral you will find the tomb of the author of the earliest surviving history of England. Who was he?

9 Which Durham market town has a museum in a huge building like a French château?
   A Peterlee
   B Barnard Castle
   C Bishop Auckland

10 Which abbey stands on Holy Island off the coast of Northumberland?

11 Which great explorer was born at Marton near Middlesbrough?

12 The vintage cars from the film *Chariots of Fire* are now on display. Where?

13 Where are 200 tractors and engines on display near Stocksfield?

14 Which great castle in Northumberland was the first English castle to succumb to gunfire?

15 On which islands do a colony of grey seals live?

16 What is the Tyne and Wear Metro?

17 What are the wild white cattle of Chillingham?

18 Where can you see nineteenth-century pumping engines at work near Sunderland?

• • •

WALES

Holyhead
Anglesey
Llandudno
Bangor
Denbigh
Caernarvon
CLWYD
Snowdonia
Wrexham
GWYNEDD
Irish Sea
Dee
Porthmadog
Dolgellau
Newtown
Cardigan Bay
Severn
Aberystwyth
Rhayader
POWYS
Cardigan
Wye
DYFED
Tywi
Brecon
Carmarthen
Monmouth
Llanelli
WEST
GWENT
Pembroke
GLAMORGAN
Rhondda
Newport
MID
Swansea
GLAMORGAN
Cardiff
SOUTH
Severn
GLAMORGAN
Bristol Channel

1 Which town is known as 'the gateway to Wales'?

2 Cader Idris is a mountain in Wales. What does it mean?
   A the seat of Idris
   B the chair of Cader
   C Castle of Rhys
   D Falling Island

3 Who built a dyke to mark the Welsh border?

4 Which is the highest mountain in Wales and England?

5 Where was water crossed by Thomas Telford and later by Robert Stephenson?

6 How did they cross it?

7 What connection is there between one of the border castles and a sleeve?

8 Which castle has the largest area next to Windsor Castle?
   A Raglan
   B White
   C Caernarfon
   D Chepstow

9 Can you name six Welsh counties?

10 What is Cadw? What does it do?

11 What is an Eistedfodd?
   A a Welsh lamb stew
   B a mountain in South Wales
   C a festival of music and speech
   D a Welsh sheep

12 What were the Romans looking for at Pumpsaint near Caernarfon?

13 St David, patron saint of Wales, is buried in St David's Cathedral. What makes the cathedral different from almost any other?

14 Where is Britain's only rack-and-pinion railway still operated by steam locomotives?

15 Wales is famed for its Great Little Railways. Can you name two?

16 It's the town in Anglesey with the longest name in the world. Can you name it . . . all?!

17 Where is the longest cable car in Britain?

18 Which castle, north of Cardiff, is known as 'Sleeping Beauty's Castle'?

19 Which of these was Britain's first stone-built castle?

   A Newport

   B Chepstow

   C Bronllys

20 Which town in North Wales has a town wall with 22 towers and three original gateways?

21 What kind of mine can you visit near Clywedog Dam in mid-Wales?

22 Which castle stands between the estuaries of Cardigan and Tremadog Bays?

23 Where does the Welsh nickname Taffy come from?

24 What is this?

25 Where is there a coracle race in August? What is a coracle?

● ● ●

NORTHERN IRELAND

Lough
Foyle

Coleraine

Bann

Derry

LONDONDERRY

Ballymena

Larne

Foyle

ANTRIM

Moume

TYRONE

Lough
Neagh

Belfast

Omagh

Newtownard

Dungannon

Lower
Lough
Erne

Portadown

Lurgan

Enniskillen

Bann

DOWN

FERMANAGH

Armagh

Upper
Lough
Erne

ARMAGH

Newcastle

Newry

1 Can you name the six counties which make up Northern Ireland?

2 What is the capital of Northern Ireland?

3 What is made of about 40,000 basalt rock columns by the sea in County Antrim? What is thought to have made it?

4 Which is the biggest lake in the United Kingdom?

5 Where do ferries from the Orkneys come to a harbour used by the Vikings?

6 Which museum has working water wheels and steam engines among much else?

7 Sugar cane and bananas growing in Belfast! Where?

8 Polar bears and penguins breeding in Belfast! Where?

9 What and where is the Giant's Ring?

10 What is Bushmills' claim to fame?

11 Where is a bridge put up each summer and taken down each autumn?

12 There is only one working windmill in Northern Ireland. Where is it?

13 The Ulster Folk and Transport Museum has reconstructed houses, a forge, a flax scrutching mill and much else. Where is it?

14 Where can you see full-scale models of Gemini and Voyager spacecraft?

15 Where was Queen Macha's Palace?

16 Which castle was abandoned when the kitchen and cooks fell into the sea?

● ● ●

OFF THE SHORES
OF SCOTLAND

SHETLAND

ORKNEY

LEWIS

HARRIS

. UIST

UIST

ISLE OF
SKYE

SCOTLAND

1 What is the joint name of the islands of Lewis, Harris and North and South Uist?

2 One of the Scottish islands is famed for its wool and its ponies. Which is it?

3 This island in the west of Scotland was the 'cradle of Christianity' in the area. Which is it?

4 Until the fifteenth century the Orkney and Shetland Islands were not part of Scotland. What nation did they belong to?

5 Which small island fits this description?
It is 107 metres (350 feet) high. It is off the coast of East Lothian. It is a bird sanctuary.

6 In the boat song, which island do you go 'over the sea' to?

7 What or who is the Old Man of Hoy?

8 Where do 8,000 gannets live on a rock surrounded by sea?

9 What are Unst, Yell and Scalloway?

10 What is the northernmost tip of the Scottish mainland called?

● ● ●

SCOTLAND

Wick

North Sea

Stornoway

Ullapool

WESTERN
ISLES

HIGHLAND
REGION

Elgin

Skye

Inverness

GRAMPIAN
REGION

Loch
Ness

Spey

Aberdeen

Dee

Fort William

TAYSIDE REGION

Tay

Dundee

Mull

Oban

Perth

St Andrews

CENTRAL
REGION

FIFE REGION

Atlantic Ocean

Loch
Lomond

Stirling

Kirkcaldy

Jura

LOTHIAN
REGION

STRATHCLYDE
REGION

Glasgow

Edinburgh

Islay

Clyde

Lanark

Galashiels

Tweed

Kintyre

Arran

Ayr

BORDERS REGION

Hawick

DUMFRIES AND
GALLOWAY REGION

Dumfries

Stranraer

1 Can you name six Scottish counties?

2 It is the highest mountain in Britain. It towers 1,343 metres (4,406 feet) near Fort William. What is it?

   A Snowdon

   B Ben Nevis

   C Cader Idris

3 Which two stretches of water are linked by the Crinan Canal?

4 What has run sea to sea at the narrowest part of Scotland since AD 143?

5 Which village has the shortest name in Britain?

6 What happened traditionally at Gretna Green?

7 What are the Honours of Scotland and where can you see them?

8 What is a croft; a crofter?

9 What is this?

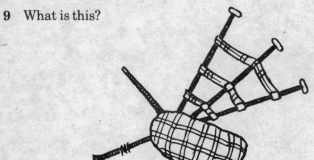

10 Different areas of Britain have different words to describe their geographical features, some of which may be special to the area. Can you match these features and definitions in Scotland?

A	wick	**1**	*stream*
B	glen	**2**	*village*
C	loch	**3**	*lake*
D	burn or beck	**4**	*valley*
E	ness	**5**	*headland*

11 What are the Grampians?

12 What was the Act of Union?

13 What is the High Kirk of Scotland in Edinburgh called?

14 Why did Edinburgh have the nickname 'Auld Reekie'?

15 Where in Glasgow can you see exhibits brought back by Captain Cook from the South Seas?

16 What, in Glasgow, is the Barras?

17 Where in Edinburgh can you see Sir Walter Scott, James Watt, James Barrie and Dr Livingstone (I presume)?

18 Where can you see the Never Never Land and a Chamber of Horrors?

19 Which important event do the monuments in the Valley of Glencoe commemorate?

20 How can subtropical gardens with palm trees flourish on the west coast of Scotland?

21 What is Loch Fyne famed for?
   A salmon
   B kippers
   C mackerel
   D smoked herring

22 Which great event takes place in Edinburgh each August?

23 Golf originated in Scotland. Where near Dundee can you see a museum devoted to its history?

24 What is and where can you see Britain's oldest ship afloat?

25 What connection has 9 Brechin Road, Kirriemuir, Angus with Kensington Gardens in London?

26 What is a cairngorm? Where can you see one weighing 24 kg (52 pounds)?

27 In which lake is a monster reputed to live?

28 Which is the largest Scottish lake?

29 What is Cameron Loch Lomond?

30 Why is Queen's View, Loch Lomond so named?

31 Which original rail bridge blew down in 1879 in a gale while a train was crossing it?

32 Which bridge spans the Atlantic?

33 Where is the Robinson Crusoe statue? Whose life suggested the story of Robinson Crusoe?

34 Who was Greyfriars Bobby and where is he remembered in Edinburgh?

35 Where can you see Sir Walter Scott and his dog, Maida?

36 Where is Macbeth said to have murdered Duncan?

37 Where is Fingal's Cave, which inspired Mendelssohn to write music named after it?

38 What is Neptune's Staircase?

39 What is special about the North Carr Lightship?

40 Which cathedral is known as 'the Lantern of the North'?

41 Why is Queensferry near Edinburgh so named?

42 What do these have in common? Glengarioch; Glen Grant; Glenlivet.

43 What is a tartan?

44 How many Scottish tartans are there?
   A   100
   B   200
   C   over 250
   D   over 300

45 Can you name the labelled parts of this Highland dress?

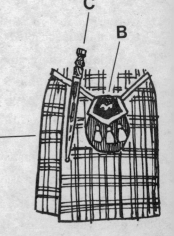

46 Flora Macdonald was the Jacobite heroine who helped Bonnie Prince Charlie to escape after his defeat at Culloden in 1746. Where is she buried?

47 What were the Jacobites?

48 Braemar is the scene of the most famous of all Highland Gatherings, for the Sovereign is its patron. What is a Highland Gathering?

49 The first suspension bridge in Britain links England and Scotland across which river?

50 The Scots have a traditional Gaelic greeting, 'Ceud mile failte'. What do you think it means?

   A Stay with us a long time.

   B Go well on your journey.

   C A hundred thousand welcomes.

   D May the blessing of God go with you.

● ● ●

Answers

PART ONE: OUT AND ABOUT

The coast

The seas around us

1. A Atlantic Ocean; B North Sea; C English Channel; D Irish Sea; E Liverpool; F Felixstowe; G Hull; H Dover; I Southampton; J Bristol

Looking out from the coast

1. North Sea
2. Irish Sea
3. English Channel
4. Straits of Dover
5. About 20 miles
6. Atlantic Ocean
7. Holland
8. Canada

Along the coast

A 4; B 7; C 6; D 3; E 1; F 2; G 8; H 5

What's in the Wash?

A 6; B 3; C 7; D 10; E 8; F 2; G 9; H 4; I 1; J 5

On the water

Ships and boats

1. The *Mary Rose*
2. Sir Francis Drake circumnavigated the world. The *Golden Hind* can be seen at Brixham, Devon.
3. England expects every man will do his duty.
4. SS *Great Britain*, the first ship to rely on a screw propeller.
5. The *Titanic*.
6. The Boat Museum, Exeter Canal.
7. National Lifeboat Museum, Bristol.
8. The Blue Peter is a naval ensign or flag, shown when a ship is about to sail.
9. A supplier of goods and equipment to ships and boats.
10. Penzance. Gilbert and Sullivan wrote an opera called *The Pirates of Penzance*.

Canals

1. An enclosed section of water for raising and lowering boats using gates fitted with sluices; a number of locks close together; a lock keeper opens and shuts lock gates to allow boats through.
2. At one time horses towed or pulled boats along the canals, walking along the towpaths.
3. Toad in *Wind in the Willows*.
4. A barge is a large, flat-bottomed boat; a narrow boat is a boat used on narrow canals; a butty is an unpowered canal boat which is towed.
5. A bridge which can be lifted to let boats through.
6. Pontysllte Aqueduct, built by Thomas Telford in 1805.
7. Manchester Ship Canal.
8. Stoke Bruerne, Northants.

9 Grand Union Canal.
10 Caledonian Canal.

Bridges and crossings

1 Stepping stones.
2 A clapper bridge.
3 A packhorse was a horse used to carry loads.
4 A toll bridge is one where you have to pay a fee to cross. Clifton Suspension Bridge in Bristol across the Avon Gorge is a toll bridge.
5 A suspension bridge.
6 A ford is a shallow place in a river where people and animals can cross; a watersplash is a place where a stream crosses over a road.
7 The Humber.
8 Tower Bridge.

Signs along the road

1 Give information.
2 Warn you of what is ahead.
3 A No entry
   B No right turn
   C Cycling prohibited
   D Overtaking prohibited
   E Speed limit 30 miles per hour
4 A Ahead only
   B Keep left
   C Roundabout ahead
   D Route for cyclists
   E Turn left ahead
5 A Crossroads
   B T-junction
   C Double bend
   D Traffic merges from left
   E Slippery road
   F Fallen or falling rocks ahead

On the road

Along the road

1 A 2; B 4; C 5; D 6; E 3; F 7; G 1; H 8
2 A major road.
3 A learner driver.
4 A bend in the road which curves one way and then another.
5 A forked road junction like a Y.
6 A 5; B 4; C 1; D 3; E 6; F 2

Road safety

1 Red—red and amber—green—green—amber—red.
2 Warns drivers of when to begin to stop or be ready to move.

On the rails

Railways

1 North Station Museum, Darlington.
2 Darlington to Bishop Auckland.
3 The Forth Railway Bridge.
4 Distance posts show how far it is from the terminus, usually found on the downline.
5 Gradient post. It shows him that there is a slope of 1 foot in 106 downhill.
6 A 5; B 2; C 4; D 6; E 3; F 1

Stations

1 D; 2 F; 3 G; 4 E; 5 C; 6 A; 7 B; 8 H

What am I wearing?

1 D; 2 H; 3 A; 4 F; 5 G;
6 E; 7 C; 8 I; 9 B; 10 J

Animals

Dog-watch

1 Boston terrier
2 Bedlington terrier
3 Airedale
4 Yorkshire terrier
5 Skye terrier
6 English setter

Animal land

1 Breeds of dairy cow
2 Breeds of beef cattle
3 Breeds of carthorse
4 Breeds of sheep
5 Breeds of hen
6 Breeds of pig
7 A cow with a band of colour around its middle.
8 Exmoor, Dartmoor, Welsh, Dales, Shetland, New Forest, Fell, Connemara, Highland.
9 A robin; B blackbird; C starling; D wren; E wagtail; F partridge
10 A Horse block: a large stone from which one mounts a horse.
   B Horse radish: a hot-tasting root used to make sauce or used in salads.
   C Horse chestnut: a large tree with pink or white blossom and large brown seeds in spiky-covered pods.

D Horsetail: a very ancient wild plant with the appearance of a green horse's tail.

Colourways

1 An open grassy area in the middle of a village.
2 South London.
3 Robin Hood.
4 Dover. They are made of whitish chalk.
5 London. Whitechapel is in the East End of London; Whitehall runs from Trafalgar Square to the Houses of Parliament in London.
6 Black Watch is a tartan and the cloth might be worn by anyone as a skirt, trousers, etc.
7 A blacksmith works with iron and shoes horses.
8 Thames.
9 The Black Country is the mining and industrial area north of Birmingham. So called because of the heavy pollution.
10 You might find blue john in Derbyshire. It is a mineral spar stone used to make ornaments.
11 Wedgwood blue is the pale blue colour used by the Wedgwood pottery.
12 A bluebell is a late spring flower.
13 An orangery is a large conservatory in which orange trees could be grown.
14 Eat it, because it is a kind of apple.
15 A bird.
16 A very famous gardener who laid out many of our great gardens.

17 The Red Arrows are the RAF flying display team.
18 No, a Red Admiral is a butterfly.
19 London.
20 Near the sea. It is a flower which grows near the shore.

Towns, cities, villages

Towns and cities

1 Oxford and Cambridge, spoken of together as old university towns.
2 Norwich, because there is a cathedral, 50 churches and 300 pubs.
3 Coventry, because he looked at Lady Godiva when she rode naked through the city in order to save her husband's life.
4 No one may speak to you.
5 Olney.
6 Blackpool.
7 Birmingham.
8 A Spa Town is a town where there are springs of medicinal waters. Among them are Leamington, Bath, Matlock, Tunbridge Wells, Harrogate, Buxton.
9 All are famous for their porcelain.
10 Birmingham.
11 Burslem, Fenton, Hanley, Longton and Tunstall.
12 Because they were the centre of the pottery industry.
13 Edinburgh.
14 Aberdeen.
15 Dundee.
16 1 D; 2 A; 3 E; 4 B; 5 F; 6 C
17 The statue of Eros, the Greek god of love.

18 A 4; B 10; C 5; D 8; E 1; F 9; G 7; H 2; I 6; J 6

Drawing places

A Gateshead
B Wick
C Appledore
D Ramsgate

How do you say . . .?

1 A   6 A
2 B   7 B
3 A   8 A
4 A   9 D
5 D   10 D

Names

Names and nicknames

1 The Irish Republic and Northern Ireland.
2 Kent.
3 Memorials to mark the places where the body of Queen Eleanor, wife of Edward I, rested each night from Nottinghamshire where she died, to Westminster Abbey where she was buried. The last is in the forecourt of Charing Cross Station.
4 A 6; B 5; C 9; D 3; E 1; F 10; G 2; H 7; I 4; J 8
5 'Of', so 'ap Ellis' means 'of Ellis', either son of Ellis or from Ellis, and 'O'Connor' means either son of Connor or from Connor.

Place names

1 A prefix is a word or syllable in front of the word which adds to or changes its meaning.

A suffix is a word or syllable at the end of a word which adds to or changes its meaning.

2–7 Check your answers by using the gazetteer of a book of maps.

8 Church beside the moor.

9 A Oxfordshire;
B Shropshire;
C Gloucestershire;
D Northamptonshire

10 They mean 'river' in local dialects.

A menu of place names

1 E; 2 H; 3 A; 4 B; 5 G;
6 C; 7 F; 8 D; 9 M; 10 I;
11 L; 12 N; 13 K; 14 J;
15 K

An ABC of place names

Appledore; Belfast; Cambridge; Dover; Edinburgh; Fishguard; Gateshead; Hastings; Inverness; Jarrow; Kingston; Llanfairpwllgwyngyll; Manchester; Norwich; Oban; Penzance; Queensferry; Redruth; St David's; Tonbridge; Ullapool; Ventnor; Westminster; Yeovil; Zennor

Questions of sport

1 1 E; 2 F; 3 G; 4 H; 5 D;
6 C; 7 B; 8 I; 9 J; 10 A

2 Horse racing.

3 A Brighton and Hove or West Bromwich
B Sheffield
C Bristol or Blackburn
D Nottingham

E Preston
F Oldham or Wigan
G Bolton or Wolverhampton
H Partick

4 Henley Royal Regatta.

5 Oxford and Cambridge boat race in the early spring.

6 Hambledon is where the first county cricket match was played.

7 A steeplechase at Aintree near Liverpool.

8 Racing across country using church steeples as landmarks.

9 Cricket.

10 A Norwich Football Club
B West Ham United
C Everton
D Southampton
E Arsenal
F Hibernian

Who lived where?

1 C; 2 F; 3 H; 4 A; 5 D;
6 J; 7 B; 8 I; 9 E; 10 G

What's that building?

1 A place where money is collected for the use of a stretch of road, a bridge or a canal.

2 A building, common in Kent, used for drying hops for beer.

3 A castle.

4 An extravagant building built entirely for decorative effect, e.g. sham castle.

5 A beehive kiln for firing pottery.

6 Cooling towers; at an electricity power station.

7 At a coal mine.

8 At the dockside.

9   A tower mill; B post mill
10 A lighthouse; it warns ships
    of dangerous waters.

Castles

1   A 10; B 5; C 6; D 9; E 8;
    F 7; G 1; H 2; I 3; J 4
2   C
3   Tower of London.
4   Dover Castle.
5   Herstmonceux in Sussex.
6   Tintagel.
7   Berkeley in Gloucestershire.
8   Warwick.
9   He was invested as Prince of
    Wales there.
10 Caerphilly.

Farming

1   A plough; B mower;
    C baler; D elevator;
    E harrow; F cultivator;
    G hay turner; H crop
    sprayer; I tractor;
    J combine harvester
2   1 F; 2 B; 3 E; 4 D; 5 H;
    6 C; 7 A; 8 I; 9 J; 10 G
3   A Dutch barn.
4   Materials added to soil to
    help plants grow.
5   A cow-house.
6   Ways of bringing water to
    crops by dug-out channels or
    pipes.
7   Cows are milked by
    machinery.
8   A wall built of large stones
    with no cement to hold them
    together.
9   A wind pump to raise water
    for the farm or sometimes to
    generate electricity.
10 A building in which silage
    (green fodder) is stored.

Stories and rhymes

1   A 2; B 7; C 10; D 1; E 9;
    F 5; G 6; H 8; I 4; J 3
2   Bowes.
3   Gloucester.
4   Sherwood Forest,
    Nottingham.
5   Castle Combe.
6   Rudyard Kipling.
7   Fort House, Broadstairs,
    Kent.
8   A dictionary maker.
9   Anne, Charlotte and Emily
    Brontë.
10 To Buckingham Palace.

Royal Britain

1   Prince Charles.
2   Silbury Hill.
3   Tintagel Abbey.
4   Corfe Castle.
5   William II (William Rufus),
    shot with an arrow while out
    hunting.
6   Eton.
7   William I (the Conqueror);
    the Royal Family.
8   Queen Mary.
9   Caernarfon Castle.
10 Caernarfon Castle. The
    King, Edward I, promised
    the Welsh a prince who
    spoke no English. They
    accepted, and he gave them
    his son.
11 Henry V.
12 The spider.
13 Stirling.
14 Holyrood House, Edinburgh.
15 Glamis Castle, near Forfar,
    Scotland.

● ● ●

PART TWO: ROUND THE REGIONS

London

Places

1 The London Stone, now set in the wall of the Bank of China, Cannon Street, in the City; distances are now measured from Charing Cross.

2 Apsley House, former home of the Duke of Wellington at Hyde Park Corner. Open to the public.

3 The Theatre Museum

4 The Planetarium.

5 As a memorial to those killed in war.

6 Hamleys, Regent Street.

7 The Geological Museum, South Kensington.

8 At the Punch and Judy public house in Covent Garden; Punch and Judy shows are quite often given in Covent Garden, near the Transport Museum.

9 Costume and fashion through the ages.

10 A stone obelisk made thousands of years ago in Egypt and given to Britain by Egypt in the nineteenth century.

11 Kew Gardens.

12 You must be born within the sound of Bow Bells, which are the church bells of St Mary-atte-Bow in the City.

Royal London

1 The Tower of London.

2 The Crown Jewels.

3 The National Maritime Museum, Greenwich.

4 Westminster Abbey.

5 Outside the Houses of Parliament, where there is a statue of him.

6 Queen Boudicca.

7 Whitehall Palace.

8 King Charles I.

9 The Royal Mews at Buckingham Palace, stables and coach houses for the Palace. These are some of the State Coaches used by the Royal Family on great occasions.

10 The Royal Standard is flying over Buckingham Palace.

11 Horse Guards Parade; the colour is the flag of the regiment showing its battle honours. It is traditionally trooped, or walked back and forth in front of the soldiers, so that they will recognize their own flag in battle.

12 Kensington Palace.

London's river

1 E

2 Look at a map of Greater London to check.

3 B

4 Thames, Tower, Rotherhithe, Greenwich Tunnel, Blackwall, Dartford.

5 From the Isle of Dogs to Greenwich by way of the Greenwich Tunnel.
6 London Bridge is now in America.
7 Tower Bridge.
8 Tower Bridge Museum.
9 The Thames Barrier near Woolwich is a series of moveable gates designed to stop surge tides from flooding London.
10 St Katharine's Dock.
11 Along the Regent's Canal.
12 HMS *Belfast* was a World War II cruiser; now a museum, it is in the Port of London.
13 The *Cutty Sark* was a 1869 tea clipper; *Gypsy Moth II* was the boat in which Sir Francis Chichester sailed single-handed around the world. They are both on show at Greenwich.
14 The history of ships.
15 The Serpentine.

London's transport

1 Transport Museum, Covent Garden.
2 Science Museum, South Kensington.
3 They are all railway terminus stations.
4 Clapham Junction.
5 At the Imperial War Musem. The Fokker E-1 was an early German fighter aircraft; a Handley Page 0/400 was the first twin-engined bomber and was in action during the First World War; the V-2 was a German World War II ballistic missile.
6 They were all World War II fighter aircraft. You can see examples at the Imperial War Museum.
7 Bus.
8 C

London's people

1 It tells you that a famous person once lived in that building.
2 A 2; B 3; C 4; D 1
3 Highgate Hill. The place is marked by a stone.
4 The Lord Mayor of London.
5 The Bank of England.
6 Gog and Magog.
7 The Yeoman Warders or 'beefeaters'.
8 Madame Tussaud's waxworks, Marylebone Road.
9 They are all buried in Poets' Corner in Westminster Abbey.
10 J. M. Barrie's Peter Pan.

London's animals

1 London Zoo, Regent's Park.
2 Ravens.
3 Mounting guard in Whitehall by Horse Guards Parade.
4 Natural History Museum, South Kensington.
5 Pelicans.
6 Crystal Palace, South London.
7 The lion, made of composition stone, that stands at the south side of Westminster Bridge.
8 Lions.

London landmarks

1 The Monument; 311 steps.
2 The Commonwealth Institute, Kensington High Street.

3   The Greenwich Meridian is an imaginary line around the globe which passes through Greenwich Royal Observatory and from which longitude is measured. You can stand with one foot on one side and one on the other and be in two areas of longitude.

4   A theatre in Islington mainly concerned with showing ballet from Britain and abroad.

5   Museum of Childhood, Bethnal Green.

6   London Toy and Model Museum, Bayswater.

7   The British Broadcasting Corporation: radio is based at Portland Place, television at White City.

8   A little over a square mile.

9   Fleet Street was famous as the centre of the newspaper industry, although many papers have moved out recently. It was named after the Fleet River, which once ran there and now runs underground.

10 Covent Garden.

11 The Chelsea Flower Show.

12 The site of the famous East End Sunday market.

13 Both are football grounds: Tottenham Hotspur's and Chelsea's.

14 The Norwegian government, to thank Britain for her help during the war.

West Country

1   Atlantic Ocean and English Channel.

2   B.

3   Cornwall.

4   They are all Cornish villages.

5   Mousehole.

6   A Cornish pixy or fairy.

7   Helston.

8   World in Miniature, Goonhaven.

9   Butterfly World, Padstow.

10 The Italian inventor Marconi sent the first radio message to America.

11 A Cornish fish pie with fish cooked whole with their heads sticking out of the pastry.

12 With Tom Cobbleigh to Widdicombe Fair at Widdicombe-in-the-Moor, Dartmoor.

13 The Pilgrim Fathers' journey to America in the *Mayflower*; a group persecuted for their religious beliefs in the seventeenth century who went to America and established New England.

14 A steam train from Buckfastleigh to Totnes.

15 Lynton.

16 C.

17 Devon.

18 D.

19 B.

20 To be a naval officer. There is a naval college there.

21 Cider.

22 Stalactites grow down; stalagmites build up.

23 Jacob's Ladder is 322 steps to the top of Cheddar Gorge, from where you can see five counties.

24 Cheddar Caves, from Madame Tussaud's Waxworks in London. The

humidity there prevents the wax from drying out.

25 The Roman baths that use the mineral springs and are still in use.
26 American Museum, Claverton near Bath.
27 Clifton Suspension Bridge, a toll bridge.
28 Avon.
29 B.
30 Yeovilton.

South of England

1 A large Iron Age fort (near Wimborne).
2 The Tank Museum, Bovington Camp, Wool.
3 C.
4 Dorchester.
5 The Isle of Purbeck is an area of land jutting out from south Dorset to the west of Poole harbour. It is a place where marble is quarried.
6 Brownsea Island, Poole Harbour.
7 They are all villages in Dorset.
8 Sherborne Castle.
9 The New Forest is common land and people have the right to graze their livestock in it.
10 The beautiful place.
11 Winchester Cathedral.
12 The Great Hall, Winchester; a record made by William the Conqueror of the land and property of the people of England in 1086.
13 Aldershot.
14 The Aldershot Military Museum.
15 Southampton; QE II stands for *Queen Elizabeth II*, the luxury cruise liner.

South East England

1 The South Downs are a range of hills running parallel with the coast from Portsmouth to Eastbourne; a breed of sheep is named after them.
2 B.
3 Channel Tunnel; by train.
4 By train, ferry, hovercraft, plane and helicopter – and some people swim!
5 Kent.
6 The White Horse of Uffington.
7 King John signed Magna Carta (the Great Charter).
8 Magna Carta gave the British people many of the basic freedoms we retain today. The site beside the Thames where the charter was signed is open to the public.
9 A, the Hog's Back is the western edge of the Downs in Surrey.
10 Wisley, Surrey; horticulture is the art of growing flowers, fruit and vegetables.
11 D.
12 The Royal Pavilion.
13 The National Museum of Penny Slot Machines in Pier Pavilion.
14 Battle Abbey.
15 The Bayeux Tapestry, in Bayeux Cathedral in France, tells the story of the Battle of Hastings in 1066 and the events leading up to it.
16 Dolphins and tropical fish, sea lions and turtles.
17 The Battle of Britain in 1940.

18 C.
19 Romney Hythe and Dymchurch Light Railway.
20 The path followed by pilgrims from Winchester to Canterbury.

Thames and Chilterns

1 B, a range of hills stretching north east from near Reading.
2 An ancient road crossing England from Dorset to the Wash.
3 The Museum of English Rural Life.
4 The Duke of Wellington.
5 Blenheim Palace; Sir Winston Churchill.
6 The Thames.
7 Bodleian.
8 The bell in the tower of Christchurch, Oxford.
9 B.
10 Banbury – at least in the nursery rhyme.
11 Banbury cakes.
12 The Ashmolean in Oxford.
13 Bekinscot.
14 Whipsnade near Dunstable, Bedfordshire.
15 The 147-metre (483-foot)-long lion marked in the chalk on Dunstable Downs.
16 A.
17 Woburn Abbey.
18 Hatfield.

East Anglia

1 Epping Forest.
2 Colchester.
3 Newmarket.
4 Bury St Edmunds. Edmund, last king of the Angles, was buried here; in 1215 the Barons swore at his shrine to make King John sign the Magna Carta.
5 As a painter.
6 Rivers in Suffolk.
7 Because the painter John Constable lived here and painted scenes in the area.
8 She was murdered and buried by her lover, William Corder. Her stepmother dreamt three times of the place where her body was discovered.
9 The Broads are a series of man-made lakes caused by people digging for peat to use as fuel.
10 D.
11 Great Yarmouth.
12 The Romans.
13 Anna Sewell, who wrote *Black Beauty*, lived there.
14 He was the first Prime Minister of Britain.
15 Lavender.
16 B.
17 Devil's Dyke.
18 Queen's College.
19 The large bay dividing Norfolk and Lincolnshire.
20 The Fitzwilliam Museum.

Heart of England

1 A range of low hills running south east to north west in Gloucestershire.
2 The Severn.
3 Wales.
4 The Avon.
5 One of the true forests left in England, in Gloucestershire.

6   C (An escarpment is a steep slope at the edge of a plateau.)
7   To see the fruit trees in blossom.
8   B, Malvern Water is a bottled spring water.
9   The Grand Union Canal.
10 Near Birmingham.
11 A.
12 Beatrix Potter's Tailor of Gloucester.
13 The Wildfowl Trust, Slimbridge.
14 The Thames.
15 D.
16 A.
17 Hereford; a collection of books fixed by chains to the shelves because they were so rare and valuable when there were very few books.
18 Ironbridge Gorge, Shropshire, over the Severn.
19 Abraham Derby first smelted iron here using coke as fuel in the eighteenth century; this led to the technology which created the Industrial Revolution.
20 Warwick Castle.
21 Kenilworth.
22 Shakespeare; Stratford-upon-Avon.
23 Shakespeare's plays are staged.
24 Birmingham City Art Gallery.
25 Lichfield in Staffordshire.
26 Alton Towers.
27 Chatterley Whitfield Mining Museum near Stoke-on-Trent.
28 Stoke-on-Trent.
29 Izaak Walton.
30 A 3; B 5; C 2; D 1; E 4

East Midlands

1   Rutland Water.
2   Rutland.
3   Lincolnshire.
4   B, Crich near Matlock in Derbyshire.
5   By cable car.
6   Woodlands, the Prospect Tower with wonderful views and the re-creation of a working lead mine.
7   Hardwick Hall; it has an unusual number of windows for its period.
8   They are all dales in Derbyshire.
9   They are both spa towns.
10 Richard Arkwright.
11 Chesterfield.
12 C; speleology is the scientific study of caves.
13 Burghley House; Burghley Three Day Horse Trials
14 Spalding.
15 Bulbs: tulips, daffodils, etc.
16 B, Lincoln.
17 The 83-metre (272-foot) tower of Boston church, a landmark in the flat countryside.
18 The Law of Gravity.
19 D. H. Lawrence.
20 A.

North West

1   The river which flows into an estuary at Liverpool.
2   D.
3   Under the Mersey via the Mersey Tunnel; over the Mersey by bridges and by the ferry to Birkenhead.
4   Beatle City, Liverpool.

5 Liverpool: one Church of England; one Catholic.
6 Higher Mill Museum, Helmshore, Rossendale and Lewis Textile Museum, Blackburn.
7 The town was built in the nineteenth century to provide homes for workers in Lord Leverhulme's soap factory.
8 On the Wirral peninsula.
9 Merseyside Maritime Museum.
10 B.
11 Isle of Man.
12 It is tailless.
13 B.
14 It is the largest water wheel in the world.
15 The grounds of Everton and Liverpool football teams.
16 Red.

Cumbria

1 Derwent.
2 Check your answer on a map.
3 They are all high points in the Lake District.
4 Windermere.
5 Wastwater.
6 Helvellyn is a 950-metre (3,118-foot) peak in the Lake District.
7 The Old Man of Coniston is a peak in the Lake District.
8 Kendal Castle.
9 The shop in Hawkshead, once owned by Beatrix Potter and now a National Trust information office.
10 The Laurel and Hardy Museum, Ulverston.
11 B.

12 The Swallows and Amazons were the children in Arthur Ransome's book of that name who had adventures particularly around the Lake District.
13 A.
14 Old entrances to Carlisle.
15 B and C.
16 Windermere Steam Boat Museum.
17 By ferry from Ulverston.
18 Characters in Beatrix Potter's books: a frog, a dog and a rabbit.

North East

1 The Pennines.
2 A dale is a valley and a fell is a hillside.
3 A.
4 The Humber Road Bridge.
5 Their name: Halifax.
6 Check on your map.
7 A long-distance path from Edale in Derbyshire northwards through Yorkshire along the Pennines.
8 Malham Tarn.
9 A, one of the largest fells in Yorkshire.
10 Pen-y-Ghent, Great Whernside and Ingleborough.
11 It carries the Settle and Carlisle railway line high above the Ribble valley.
12 It is the highest inn in England.
13 Airedales and Swaledales.
14 D.
15 A.
16 Fountains Abbey.
17 They are all abbeys.

18 They are all castles or towns with castles.
19 King Harold defeated the invading Danes.
20 Castle Howard.
21 Nunnington Hall.
22 Flamingo Land, Kirby Misperton.
23 North Yorkshire Moors Railway from Pickering to Grosmount.
24 B, York Minster.
25 Dick Turpin; the Castle Museum.

Northumbria

1 The Roman Wall – Hadrian's Wall, built to keep out the Scots and the Picts.
2 Roman camps on the Wall.
3 Carvoran, The Roman Army Museum.
4 The Cheviots.
5 South and North Tyne.
6 It is the largest waterfall in England.
7 Durham Cathedral.
8 The Venerable Bede.
9 B.
10 Lindisfarne Priory.
11 Captain Cook.
12 Newburn Hall Motor Museum, near Newcastle.
13 Hunday National Tractor and Farm Museum.
14 Bamburgh, in the fifteenth century.
15 Farne Islands.
16 The light railway which provides transport within Newcastle and district.
17 A herd descended from primeval aurochs at Chillingham Park (not to be approached without a guide!).

18 Ryhope Engines Museum.

Wales

1 Abergavenny.
2 A.
3 Offa.
4 Snowdon.
5 Menai Straits.
6 By their bridges.
7 Raglan is a castle and also a wide sleeve.
8 C.
9 Check on a map.
10 Cadw is the Welsh equivalent of English Heritage. It cares for the Ancient Monuments, such as the castles, of Wales.
11 C.
12 Gold.
13 It is built in a hollow and you climb down 39 steps to reach it.
14 Snowdon Mountain Railway, Llanberis.
15 Ffestiniog: Portmadog to Ffestiniog.
Welsh Highland Railway: Portmadog to Pen-y-Mount.
Talyllyn: from Tywyn to Snowdonia.
16 Llanfairpwllgwyngyllgogerychwyrndrobwllllantysiliogogogoch (. . . phew!).
17 Llandudno to Great Orme Headland.
18 Castle Coch.
19 B.
20 Conway.
21 Lead mine.
22 Harlech.
23 River Taff.
24 A Welsh love spoon.
25 On the River Teifi; it is a circular boat with a wicker frame covered in skin.

Northern Ireland

1 Armagh, Antrim, Down, Fermanagh, Londonderry and Tyrone.
2 Belfast.
3 The Giant's Causeway; volcanic activity.
4 Lough Neagh.
5 Stromness.
6 Ulster Museum, Belfast.
7 Botanic Gardens, Belfast.
8 Belfast Zoo.
9 A Neolithic ceremonial site near Belfast.
10 It is the world's oldest legal distillery.
11 The Carrick-a-Rede Bridge west of Ballycastle is used for fishermen during the fishing season.
12 Ballycopeland, Co. Down.
13 Cultra Manor, Hollywood.
14 The Planetarium, Armagh.
15 Navan Fort, Armagh.
16 Dunluce, near the Giant's Causeway.

Off the shores of Scotland

1 The Hebrides.
2 Shetland.
3 Iona.
4 Norse.
5 Bass Rock.
6 Skye.
7 A 137-metre (450-foot)-high isolated stone stack or pillar off north west Hoy.
8 Bass Rock – again.
9 Shetland Islands.
10 John O'Groats.

Scotland

1 Check your answer on a map.
2 B.
3 The Sound of Jura and Loch Fyne.
4 The Antonine Wall, which marked the northern limit of Roman Britain in AD 143. It runs from Bo'ness on Forth to Old Kilpatrick on Clyde.
5 Ae in Dumfries and Galloway, built by the Forestry Commission in 1947.
6 Young English people could run away across the border to be married by the local blacksmith without their parents' consent.
7 The sceptre, sword and crown of Scotland; on show in Edinburgh Castle.
8 A croft is a small highland farm; a crofter is a person who farms a croft.
9 A bagpipe. It is a musical instrument with an air bag and pipes.
10 A 2; B 4; C 3; D 1; E 5
11 A range of hills north of Dundee.
12 The Act of Union (1707) made England and Scotland one country.
13 St Giles' Cathedral.
14 Because it was so smoky and foggy.
15 The Hunterian Museum.
16 A weekend market.
17 The Edinburgh Wax Museum.
18 The Edinburgh Wax Museum.
19 The massacre of Glencoe on

13 February 1693, when government troops under Archibald Campbell killed 38 Macdonalds for being late in coming to pay allegiance to William III.

20 Because the warm waters of the Gulf Stream bring a mild climate to this area.

21 Smoked herring or kippers.

22 The Edinburgh Festival and Military Tattoo.

23 Spaling Golf Museum, Camperdown, Dundee.

24 The Frigate *Unicorn*, at Victoria Dock, Dundee.

25 James Barrie, author of *Peter Pan*, was born here. The statue of Peter Pan is in Kensington Gardens.

26 A yellow or maroon semi-precious stone named for the mountain in Scotland where it is mainly found; Braemar Castle, Aberdeen.

27 Loch Ness.

28 Loch Lomond.

29 A wildlife park near Balloch on Loch Lomond.

30 Queen Victoria had her first view of Loch Lomond from this spot in 1879.

31 The Tay Bridge.

32 Clachan Bridge links the island of Seil near Oban to the mainland, over an inlet of the Atlantic Ocean.

33 Lower Laergo; Andrew Selkirk (1676–1721).

34 A Skye terrier who watched over his master's grave from 1858 for fourteen years. His statue is in the Kirk of Greyfriars, Edinburgh.

35 The Scott Monument, Princes Street, Edinburgh.

36 Cawdor Castle.

37 Island of Staffa; Mendelssohn's *Fingal's Cave*.

38 A flight of locks on the Caledonian Canal, built 1805–22, which raised the water level 20 metres (64 feet).

39 A floating museum, giving a real impression of life on a lightship.

40 Elgin.

41 After the eleventh-century Queen Margaret, who used the ferry between Dunfermline and Edinburgh.

42 All are malt whiskies.

43 A Scottish woollen fabric woven with crossing stripes, traditionally showing patterns of the clans.

44 C.

45 A Kilt; B Sporran; C Dirk.

46 Kilmuir, Isle of Skye.

47 The followers of James Stewart, father of Bonnie Prince Charlie.

48 A sports meeting with competitions for tossing the caber, races and highland dancing.

49 Tweed.

50 C.

● ● ●